L(

Addicted to Brightness

POETS
Fiona Benson
Rachael Boast
Jen Hadfield
Edwin Morgan
Raman Mundair
Don Paterson
Robin Robertson

EDITORS
Sophy Dale
Alan Warner

Long Lunch Press
2006

Addicted to Brightness

Unless otherwise stated, the copyright for all poems remains with the authors © 2006. The authors have asserted their rights under the Copyright, Designs and Patents Act, 1988, to be identified as authors of this work.

Limited edition of 500 copies.

Published by:
Long Lunch Press
Sandeman House, Trunk's Close, 55 High Street,
Edinburgh, EH1 1SR

in association with Scottish Book Trust.

Typesetting and internal page design by Cluny Sheeler.
Cover design by James Hutcheson.
Printed and bound by InType Libra Ltd, London.

Published with the assistance of a grant from the Scottish Arts Council.

A CIP record is available from the British Library

0 9554650 0 1 (10-digit ISBN)
978 0 9554650 0 0 (13-digit ISBN)

LIST OF CONTENTS

	Acknowledgements
1	Preface
5	Rachael Boast
15	Don Paterson
19	Fiona Benson
29	Edwin Morgan
33	Raman Mundair
39	Robin Robertson
41	Jen Hadfield
57	Biographical Notes

ACKNOWLEDGEMENTS

Great thanks to Gavin Wallace at the Scottish Arts Council, all the writers who contributed to this and future booklets, and especially Don Paterson, Robin Robertson and Michael Ondaatje – who tried to get something underway, but was deeply immersed in editing. Thanks to John Burnside, Irvine Welsh, Janice Galloway, Louise Welsh and Annie Proulx; and to Marc Lambert, Lilias Fraser, Liz Small, Jenny Vass, James Robertson and Elaine at Word Power bookshop. Thanks also for inspiration down the years to Kevin Williamson, Duncan Glen of Akros Press and of course to Mr Duncan McLean. A special warm thanks to Edwin Morgan.

PREFACE

Allow me to show you to your table. The Long Lunch Press has come about largely under the inspiration of novelist and short story writer Duncan McLean's Clocktower Press which he started up in 1990. The odd bottle too many and the Rebel Inc dialectic taints us also. You can read more about those influential presses and the work they published in *Ahead of its Time* (Vintage). Sophy Dale – the brains and grace of the Long Lunch Press – and I had talked for years about attempting a small something to assist 'emerging' writers based in Scotland. My only use was to persuade some 'established' writers to contribute new work to combine with the fresh produce. We decided to publish only five or six booklets in limited editions, roughly two a year, pay the bill and leave, tipping heavily. This has more or less gone to plan. Sadly we will not be able to consider any more contributions from new writers. (Established ones being another matter). I was heartened how quickly we found really good work from new writers. Many were from creative writing groups – my notions about the virtues of slaving away alone in a room are clearly to do with personal psychology.

The early '90s for me was an exciting and very different time to be first published in. It was all electric typewriters, lack of professionalism and no thought of tomorrow. I was awful lucky and always knew it. I recall in 1992 buying the Clocktower Press booklet, *Parcel of Rogues*, for £1.99 from Waterstones on Princes St, Edinburgh. Inside its stapled pages there were early versions of James Kelman's, *How Late It Was, How Late*, Janice Galloway's *Foreign Parts* and a sequence from an unpublished novel, called *Trainspotting At Leith Central Station*. Within a year I was contributing to Clocktower myself and my own first novel was accepted for publication. Enough said. It would be impossibly foolish for Long Lunch or any other small press to have such influential ambitions. We just hope to get the work of some new, Scottish-based writers started on their road and to enjoy the accomplishment of great writers we admire. We were also adamant we would pay all our writers an encouraging and identical fee – a luxury the Clocktower Press could never have considered. Early blinkers for the penury to come! We're also especially pleased for our hors-d'oeuvre to be of recent Scottish poetry, not lip service but an admission it is the art form most overlooked in Scotland and elsewhere by the latest Sunday

PREFACE

Supplement Zeitgeist. Not in our kitchens! Pride is a rare feeling these days but I'm proud of what everyone has achieved here. Next we have a menu including several tempting booklets of short stories and exciting novel extracts. And I know I'll still fancy a chip supper on the way home.

Alan Warner, October 2006

Rachael Boast

FALLS OF INVERSNAID

I doubt we could say now
that the water thunders down,

but rather, beginning at some spot
of rockrose, moss and bracken,

it *believes*, cannot do other
than turn towards its larger cause

and, from scintillate wit and flaunt
around the dark roll of rock,

come to serve the steadier life,
bringing the over and above back down

to where they have meaning
for us – cloud and mountain mood

made equable in the same calm mirror –
until we lose ourselves again

in the lift and fall of the water,
its let-be and lintel of light.

AVENUE OF LIMES

The whole place is bushed-out –
mid-July heat and equipoise bodied
in the aphid's meticulous frenzy,
the song-radar of the blackbird,

and the lime tree leaves
faint with chlorophyll, bending
like rods for the cool green
tint of the streaming air.

I call out to them:
By-standing trouble-shooters,
Upholders of the peace,
Seraphim of the long gravel path.

And for once I'm off the hook,
unscrutinized,
given the all-clear,
malaise lifting under the hush.

BUNKHOUSE

The evening rain, staccato against
the slope of the window,
rehearses for another downpour
bringing the backpackers in to rest.
What presses on me is this:
we have to walk a long way
before the cloud comes down to meet us.

Glinn Chrochte, the hanging valleys
of Nevis. I could almost draw
the line here, go no further,
take back the southern lush
of Bristol; tell myself we find
where we belong by first being lost.
But this steep drop –

this vertiginous longing –
asks me to look beyond
the scree and peat of it
into annals and emblems:
sword and turret,
the stag head
mounted on the wall above the bar –

to imagine growing entwined
herald and threat of antler,
the come-on and the back-off,
to be self-possessed,
carrying nothing,
to bow bone-lightning down
in bog-cotton.

REDCLIFF QUAY

The waves, punctual, lucid, river-tongued,
tug at the hulks of the boats.

Out on the terrace of the Waterside Café,
there's a man who's not the same man

he was when walking the street.
Here he gains in presence,

a distinguished guest, undulant
above the silt-line of coffee cups –

St. Mary's delivers up her bell-canticle –
he lends a hand to his hair in the high wind

that carries a wave of light diagonally
from quayside to quayside.

Mid-river, two mute swans
dip-down, disappear, re-appear,

sun-dazzled and dripping light.
They fix each other with serious eyes,

form a heart of white necks,
knowing with fierce clarity

when to become unseen, when to seek
out the chamber of the moment,

its floating chandelier, bright invisibility,
until she's submerged

beneath his meat-weight,
his coarse, vocal reverberation.

Standing on the near-side,
I'm taken with the water's louche

posture, the slab and tilt of it,
and somehow built up again bodily,

from blood-burn, silver-scale and sallow.
Thoughts arise in parallel with the all-seeing,

all-saying world made word, as though this
were a sonal, glass-hulled boat,

steering between mudflats that glisten and flag
the stark estuary of the Severn.

Don
Paterson

THE POETRY
after Li Po

I found him wandering on the hill
one hot blue afternoon.
He looked as skinny as a nail,
as pale-skinned as the moon;

below the broad shade of his hat
his face was cut with rain.
My God . . . poor Tu Fu, I thought:
It's the poetry again.

Fiona
Benson

EMMAUS

And if you should forget
walk out across the Hungerford Bridge
where the city falls back

and pylons loom in the dark
like an avenue of silver birch.
Regard the work:

a simple stitch, it heals
the breach of the river, allows passage and pause
to acknowledge our place

beneath this infinite sky
in a wind that knows we are mortal, porous,
a beautiful trick of the light.

BURRS

Beneath the hiss and lash
of bramble arms
binding the path,

the low moan of stalks
unburdening themselves
at the drag of my hem

with something like pain;
their silent freight
gnaws at my coat,

winds its hooks in the cloth;
I plant a waste-ground
when I tear them off.

HARVEST

All August rain, then summer's heat;
now this unbearable weight –
pears dissolve on the branch,
the orchard's glut of apples and plums
rots in the grass.

Out here where we walk
it's hips and haws,
brambles that loosen in the sun,
blacken into full bloom,
become juice on the stalk.

I taste all this on your tongue
as, dragged down to the wet ground,
we waste ourselves again,
lost to the summons of this old need,
this flaring into thistledown; pod, bract, seed.

UNACCOMPANIED

It's raining at the garden centre.
I walk through dripping aisles of potted herbs
in a cool green rinse of aniseed and catmint.

The water falls in diatonic intervals –
each drop calls out its one clear note
as the canopy of leaves sings counterpoint.

I want you here to listen that way you do
with your eyes half-closed and mouth a little tense,
but don't come and get you. Instead, I rehearse

this trick of solitary listening
against the time you leave, like a beginner
at piano with the practice pedal down

crawling a way through the minor scale
until my fingers have it blind.
But, like listening with one ear sealed,

it misses a dimension, or depth of sound . . .
the rain taps shallow as a glockenspiel,
an infant music, untutored and unreal.

FISHERWIFE SANG

We focht afore the viage;
skelpt, strushled, bit
for him oot bousin
while a wapt his nets.

Whan a cadged him oot tae the boat
he knidged ma heid,
made hiself weichtie as the deil
willed me tae faw

but a helt strang,
let ma maucht traivel doun
throu jaw and saun
and earthed in the stane.

A gied him his stap up
then wyded back,
didnae bide tae see him aff.
Ill luck tae pairt like that.

A sleepit wi ma face
tae the waw and wadna greet
but wis waiting on shore
whan they retourned the neist week.

Ma man lowpt aff the boat
his herr steive wi saut
slunged throu the swaw
and claucht me up.

We wir culyin an cruinin
richt there in the watter
than lookt at ilk ither
and ran.

He was unner ma claes
gin we'd gat hame;
afore the door closed
a wis hoised round his waist

him inower,
the baith o us lilting thegither.

TENTSMUIR

The Arctic Terns are back.
They come for the light,
chasing Summertime
from the Antarctic to here,

addicted to brightness
that drags at the throat
and never lets fall,
while all the while

Winter's stain
chases at their heels.
I watch one with its black eyes
like the puncture of a snakebite

scanning for fish.
It snatches at the water
then draws back, scalded
by loneliness that haunts there.

WAYS OUT

There's this gang of swifts down Lamond Drive
carving up the light, a cull of flies.
The Reader's Digest Book of British Birds says
they come down to earth less and less,
conceive in mid-air, that at dusk they spiral up
for miles, then nap on thermals, snatching sleep
in the freefall. They have cast off land habits
like excess baggage, and are helpless on the ground
near-crippled by their shrivelled claws. Perhaps
one day they will escape entirely, slip
the noose of gravity, its trip-wire snared
on a feather. My own departures are short-lived.
I look to cut loose and cannot leave.

Edwin Morgan

1955 – A RECOLLECTION

> First there was one,
> then there were two,
> now there is one,
> when will there be none?

Step down slowly,
down into the cold,
old cold, eternal cold,
refrigerated cold,
with grim stiff guards
every few feet
even in their greatcoats
cold, cold –
our shuffling queue
silent, shivering,
awed a little,
believers and unbelievers
circling a shrine,
curious, peering,
cameras forbidden,
eyes and brain

fixing images
that startle, frighten,
fascinate finally –
the two undead
laid side by side,
Lenin yellowing,
showing his years,
Stalin still rosy
as if lightly sleeping –
the strangest tableau
you are likely to see
this side of the grave.
I pour the amber
of a poem over it.

> First there was one,
> then there were two,
> now there is one,
> when will there be none?

Raman Mundair

SHETLAND MUSE

Outside dark molasses
absorbs the last juice
from a misshapen tangerine
and pours it thick across the vale.
The wind furious at being
ignored whips the ocean into a roar.

Soon, the gloaming begins
and something in my lower back
stirs and, later, something
lying beneath my skin moves
and my hand casts spells
that appear garbled on the page.

Throughout the night, the moon,
just out of reach, plays with the sheep;
hide and seek. Their bustle torsos
a strange comfort in a landscape
void of trees. And while most sleep
my ink, luminous, marks magic true.

STORIES FAE DA SHOORMAL (4)

Here, you hae ta be waatchful.
Nordern lichts happen
when you're sleepin.
Whaals sail by,
oot a sicht ahint ferries, tankers.
Be ever alert,
meteor shooers cascade
ahint your back, whispers
echo alang da esplanade,
transparent lives – while da days
pass, markit be *Da Shetland Times*.

STORIES FAE DA SHOORMAL (5)

Dis toon is no big anoff fur dee
ta loss desel, ta hadd dee
dis toon is no big anoff.
But it's peerie enoff ta echo
aa dy past lives; scremmin
fae every coarner, remindin dee
du wis wance
wan o da promisin' eens.
Du lassoed dy tongue an
Shaepit him inta a "sooth mooth"
an knapped desel raa,
dy lugs prunkit fir approval.
Du becam da wan
destined ta geng far.
Noo, riggit in black
lik a *Reservoir Dug*, du
veils desel in da English
wroucht, wry wit, while
aroond dee, shadows
hing fae nooses.

THE MORNING AFTER

Awake at 6, a sweet taste
in my mouth and full
of poems. The train
to Greenock, every tree
        reached out
to stroke my face.

Robin Robertson

ACTIVITY GROUP, CHRISTCHURCH AIRPORT

One does the back-crawl. Another
combs her hair, compulsively,
watching her friend waving at planes.
They have thick sloping shoulders,
submerged necks; all wear
the same shell-suits and trainers,
but each has a different colour of Walkman.
The sobbing girl sits next
to the boy who laughs at everything.
Their movements are sudden
and inaccurate: an abrupt flexion
which seems almost accidental;
hands clap themselves.
Because their tongues are too big for their heads
they seem to be concentrating.
The most damaged
are the least noticeable;
they seldom move,
don't cling to the group leaders.
Their eyes, though, are going like crazy.
Everyone is happy, waiting for the flight,

even the sobbing girl
sunk on her stomach
learning the breast-stroke, the crash-dive.
Each of them
has a plastic bottle of Coke
the size of an aqualung.

Jen Hadfield

GUSTER

At dusk I walked to the postbox,
and the storm that must've passed you earlier today
skirled long, luminous ropes of hail between my feet
and I crackled in my waterproof
like a roasting rack of lamb.

And across the loch,
the waterfalls blew right up off the cliff
in grand plumes like smoking chimneys.

And on the road
even the puddles ran uphill.

And across Bracadale,
a gritter, as far as I could tell,
rolled a blinking ball of orange light
ahead of it, like a dungbeetle
that had stolen the sun.

And a circlet of iron was torn from a byre
and bowled across the thrift.

And seven wind-whipped cows
clustered under a bluff.

And in a rockpool
a punctured football reeled around and around.

And even the dog won't walk since yesterday
when – sniffing North addictedly –
he saw we had it coming –

and I mean more'n weak wet hail
on a bastard wind.

SNUSKIT

The shore is just not nice. Good. The hashed basalt is black and all the rubberduckery of the Atlantic is blown up here to endure for ever and aye etcetera: a bloated seal and sometimes skull, fishboxes and buoys, a cummerbund of rotting kelp. The wind topples me, punches me gently into a pool. Beyond, strafed with hail, the sea teems like a TV with a frayed aerial. The wind punches me gently into a pool. I step back onto my tuffet, boots pooled in buttery light. The wind punches me gently into a pool. I'm doing my best impression of a gull: pesky, pitied, lonely, greedy, hopping up and down on my tuffet. The wind punches me gently into a pool.

HÜM

(*for Bo*)

Twilight, gloaming;

to walk blind
against the wind;

to be abject; lick snot
and rain from the top lip
like a sick calf.

To be blinded by rain
from the north.

To be blinded
by westerly rain.

To walk uphill
into a tarry peatcut
and bluster a deal with the Trowes.

To cross the bull's field
in the dark.

To pass in the dark
a gate of hollow bars
inside which the wind is broaling.

To pass in the dark
a byre like a rotten walnut.

To not know the gate
til you run up against it.

NO SNOW FELL ON EDEN

There was no snow in Eden as I remember it.

There was no snow, so no thaw or *tao* as you say;
no snowmelt drooled down the brae,
baring what it should've left kindly hidden.

No yellow ice choked bogbean.
There were no sheepskulls in the midden.

It was no allotment, Eden –
but a hothouse, an orangery,
with maidenhair strummed
by a mumbling monkey.

There was no cabbage-patch of rich, roseate heads.
There was no innuendo and no snow.

No footprint thawed to the sloppy paw of a yeti.

And since in Eden they were so mature,
a steaming bing of new manure was just not funny.

Eve knew no-one who was dying.
Adam never sat up late, drinking and crying.

And if at four the sky split like a watermelon,
soddening the land with blue and citrine,
and the drowned ground wept smells,
no-one stood stock staring still.

Black was not so sooty, as I remember it.

Green was not so greeny browny.

No wheelhouse twirled redly
on an eyepopping sea.

SPELL / SEAL

On the oilboat's swell
the kelpstalks stretch and sniff and sag

and sling his throat
with gentle nooses.

The seal is dressed
in his visiting best –

throat stacked with chins like quoits,
borrowed coat of handsome dapples.

He gives a cough – tubercular.
He snorts a drag of addictive air.

Slop-slop!
goes the viscous sea into rockpools

        slop-slop!

into crusted vats
of anemone and wrack.

He takes his plashy parole.
He chucks a long luxurious roll.

SOME ROCKPOOLS

Jellyfish
medusae – babes
in the wood, with milky domes
and faint fontanelles;

constellations that
someone shook into the sea,
orphan, circlet of

fangs, spasming; a
mussed map of heavens, thimbles
on the tide's slow thumbs

Denouement
across the rockpool's frilled theatre,
a limpet budges
a devastating millimetre

The Slack of the Tide
in a slow birl of skirts
from his/her hut,
the seasnail wells
like the Widow Twankey, but

a hermit crab kens best, doesn't he?
when he chucks his commando roll
and closes with his velvet paws
the porthole of his cell.

Nature Study
She knits salted tapwater
with puzzled antennae;

unpacks a banana bunch of claws,
her googly green haversack of roe,
and last – fascination and woe –

her kernel,
a trailing corkscrew quiff of tail,
to waft, softly noughted,
at the bottom of the pyrex bowl.

HARRY HUDGEY

He beats in my hands like a soiled heart
and stippling my cupped palms,
he breathes –

flinching, cinching his perimeter in
like a kidney hitting a hot griddle;

a very small Hell's Angel
in his spiked jacket and undershirt of faint hair;
peeled from the verge
of a sweet, wet morning.

Drunk, I coddle him like a crystal ball,
hellbent the realistic mysteries
should amount to more
than guesswork and fleas.

CABBAGE

I ask the garden to bear me witness –
but what the ground mutely hands me as evening comes
looks most of all like a snoozing face –
whorled, shut, deaf to disgrace –
a mute Om from a drill of Oms,
cool and creaking – a northern lotus.

Biographical Notes

FIONA BENSON
Fiona Benson has had poems published in *The Feminist Review*, *Areté*, *The TLS*, *Oxford Poetry Broadsides* and *The Tall Lighthouse Review*, and has been given a 2006 Eric Gregory Award by the Society of Authors. She is currently trying to finish her PhD on Ophelia as a dramatic type in the early modern period, and has just moved from Anstruther to Exeter.

RACHAEL BOAST
Rachael Boast was born in Suffolk in 1975. After completing a degree in English and Philosophy at Wolverhampton University in 1996, she moved to Bristol where she lived for nine years, able to give her time to writing as a result of medical complications. In 2005 she moved to Scotland and has since completed an M.Litt in Creative Writing at St. Andrews University. She currently lives in Edinburgh and is working on a PhD.

JEN HADFIELD
Jen Hadfield stays in Burra, Shetland, where she was recently a writer in residence for Shetland Arts Trust. Her first collection *Almanacs* was published by Bloodaxe Books in 2005 and won an Eric Gregory Award that

BIOGRAPHICAL NOTES

enabled her to travel in Canada for fifteen months. She is currently working in the Bonhoga Gallery and on her second poetry manuscript, *Nigh-no-Place*. In September she took part in Nordic Connections – a celebration of Shetland, Faroese and Iceland writing – with a trip to Torshavn and Reykjavik.

Jen is also an artist and photographer. Her website is at http://www.rogueseeds.co.uk

EDWIN MORGAN

Born Glasgow in April 1920, Morgan has lived in Glasgow all his life, except for service in the Middle East during the Second World War, and his poetry is grounded in the city. He retired from Glasgow University as titular Professor of English in 1980, serving as Glasgow's first Poet Laureate 1999-2002.

The title of his 1973 collection, *From Glasgow to Saturn*, suggests the range of Morgan's subject matter. He has an international reputation, not only as a poet, but also as a critic and translator. In 2004 the Scottish Executive appointed Edwin Morgan as the first 'Scots Makar', in effect Scotland's poet laureate.

RAMAN MUNDAIR

Raman Mundair is a writer and artist. She was born in India and has lived across the UK but feels most at home in the Shetland Islands. Currently Raman is a Scottish Arts Council Writing Fellow based in Glasgow. As a playwright she was awarded a mentorship with the Playwrights Studio Scotland in 2005 and recently collaborated with the National Theatre Scotland Young Company on *Side Effects*, a one act play which opened at the Oran Mor, Glasgow and toured to Edinburgh and Dublin. Her play *The Algebra of Freedom* will be produced by 7:84 Theatre Company in 2007. In 2006 she was awarded runner up in the Penguin Decibel prize for short fiction. Raman is the author of *Lovers, Liars, Conjurers and Thieves* (Peepal Tree Press) and *A Choreographer's Cartography*, to be published by Peepal Tree Press in Spring 2007.

DON PATERSON

Don Paterson was born in Dundee in 1963. He works as a musician and editor, and teaches at the University of St Andrews. He has written five collections of poetry: *Nil Nil, God's Gift to Women* (winner of the both the T. S. Eliot Prize and the Geoffrey Faber Memorial

Prize), *The Eyes* and *Landing Light* (winner of the Whitbread Prize for Poetry and the T.S. Eliot Prize). His latest collection is *Orpheus* (Faber). He is also the author of *The Book of Shadows* (Picador).

ROBIN ROBERTSON

Robin Robertson is from the north-east coast of Scotland. *A Painted Field* won a number of awards, including the 1997 Forward Prize for Best First Collection and the Saltire Scottish First Book of the Year Award. His second collection, *Slow Air*, was published in 2002. In 2004 he received the E.M. Forster Award from the American Academy of Arts and Letters. *Swithering* won the 2006 Forward Prize for Best Collection and is shortlisted for the T.S. Eliot Prize.

FUTURE PUBLICATIONS FROM LONG LUNCH PRESS

For more information on Long Lunch Press authors and forthcoming publications, please see our webpage on the Scottish Book Trust site: www.scottishbooktrust.com

In 2007 we will be publishing three further volumes, featuring work from, amongst others, Richard Todd, Irvine Welsh, David Aitchison, Jason Donald, Elizabeth Reeder and Annie Proulx.